To Debb

THE
ROUSTABOUT
HEART

Adventures in Recovery

Hope is a gift we give to ourselves.

Mary Killian

Mary Killian

Published in the United States of America by

Tiltawhirl Press, 2015

ISBN: 978-0-9965890-0-0

Printed in the United States of America

Parties at our house always started out with the best intentions. They just ended rough.

My parents didn't know any better. Neither did I.

Do any of us, really?

This book is dedicated to my mom
and dad, Mary and Gene Dall.

I don't think either of my folks ever fully
understood my sobriety, but that doesn't mean
they weren't happy about it.

I am glad for and grateful to:

Dave Killian. As husbands go, you are my ideal. It's reassuring to know that as time passes, you remain distinctly fond of me.

Nancy Miles. Your love reminds me how much I enjoy being a daughter.

Maureen Ryan Griffin. You've helped me realize that I never want to stop writing. So I'll just keep doing it. Putting my thoughts on paper feels like something really important.

Kara Konrad. Life can be complicated, but our relationship is simple. And therapy is awesome.

Mr. David Sedaris. Your collection of essays, *Me Talk Pretty One Day*, was the first book I purchased when I got sober. I remember how relieved I was that I could still read. I'd been worried.

Claire Nonnon O'Sullivan. I miss you, and I wish you hadn't left so soon. We were just getting started.

Thank you.

Introduction

Roustabouts follow the circus train wherever it goes.

Theirs is a dirty, dangerous job. They carry heavy equipment and set up the tents for the Greatest Show on Earth. Rousting is in their blood. Yet in their hearts, there is a longing for something more than just an ordinary existence. This was true for me.

The world needs rousties because everyone loves entertainment. The world needs me, but no longer for the same reason.

I wrote *The Roustabout Heart* because I wanted to try and explain what it feels like to celebrate a life beyond addiction.

Getting clean is a lot of work, but staying thankful is the tricky part. Gratitude is the key to my enthusiastic recovery.

I appreciate all the smart and straightforward lessons I'm learning along the way. Plus, it's fun to share what I know.

I hope these simple thoughts will encourage and inspire you in helpful ways as you consider and explore your own intimate experiences with sobriety and life on life's terms.

I also wrote this book because I thought it would be so cool to write a book. I was right. It really is. ☺

It's hard to begin with the end in mind. To develop a clear picture of what I want my life to look like. To decide what my values are and set goals, like I actually know what I'm doing.

I'm not that smart or disciplined. I get caught up in trifling nonsense. I am intimidated by folks who look like they have their acts together. I google the silliest shit and watch YouTube videos about funny animals and zit popping when I should be working. I am easily distracted by music and the sound of people laughing.

Sometimes when I feel overwhelmed, I whisper God's name. It's a simple act of faith that opens a window in my heart. It lets the fresh air in so I can concentrate. It reminds me that He's always eager to help me make sense of things.

I don't have to take on the whole world in one fell swoop. I can start small with what I hope to see happen this week. Or today. Or right this minute.

When I keep my objectives simple, I can accomplish more than I realize.

I sleep soundly almost as soon as I go to bed. When my eyes open in the morning, I'm ready to flame on. For me, this remains one of the most rewarding miracles of sobriety.

I used to be awake all night, creeping around while everyone else in the world slept. I promised myself I'd get some rest, but I couldn't. I just kept hitting it—like a robot. The drinking, the pills. I couldn't stop.

Through recovery, I recognize the importance of adequate rest, the beauty of routine and the benefits of some healthy structure in my life.

Sleep helps all processes work efficiently. In slumber, my brain and body prepare for the next day. So I can learn things and remember information, solve my own problems and control my emotions.

I'm not afraid of the nighttime anymore.

I looked around the room. I watched the way they carried themselves. How easily they smiled and joked with one another. Sensitive, yet self-assured. I wanted what they had. I wasn't certain what that was.

I studied everyone closely and checked myself for big and subtle changes. I didn't know what to expect or if anything was actually happening. I hated when they said, "Keep coming back." I didn't like being told what to do.

But I did, nonetheless. I kept showing up to those early meetings, when nothing in my life made sense. I wanted to learn more. I didn't understand much.

The more I learned, the more I got it. How to get it. What it is that I truly need.

My mind is a warehouse of thoughts and ideas. I stock the shelves with intellectual merchandise.

Through recovery, I'm outgrowing the need to suffer. Little by little, I replace the chaos with peaceful experiences. They're becoming a part of my natural inventory.

I turn to these resources as I continue to rebuild my life.

I was always waiting for my life to start. To change. To improve.

With a drink in my hand and a belly full of pills, I expected the world to give me what I needed. To fix my problems. And when it didn't, to leave me alone.

Life is very different now. Thank you, God, for showing me this new freedom. For leading me toward my real happiness.

I was eager to be sexual. I wanted closeness, and I thought that was how I could get it. I was also afraid and unsure of myself. I never said 'no.'

Drinking helped alleviate my inhibitions, and drugs gave me confidence. Cocaine, speed and alcohol became the switch that turned me on and off. Eventually, I couldn't do anything without them. That's when I really started making a mess of things.

I chose boyfriends who drank and got high. When they hassled me about my drinking and drug use, I became secretive. My fear and self-consciousness returned.

This is my third marriage. My husband is neither an addict nor an alcoholic, but I am both. Our relationship has survived my addictions and long-term recovery. I realize how fortunate I am.

In sobriety, I have come to understand desire and genuine intimacy. I am no longer physically driven by loneliness. I respect my needs and those of my partner. I listen to the messages my body sends me, and I respond like the thoughtful, caring adult I know I can be.

I had myself convinced I was enhancing my subconscious thoughts whenever I got high. That I was taking my mind on these exotic trips most ordinary brains weren't special enough to enjoy. Because I was artistic and imaginative and inspired. What a load of horseshit that was.

Truth is, my addiction suffocated any potential for creativity I might have had. It was threatened by all other interests. Art requires effort, and at the very least, an ability to respond to things emotionally.

I'm sure I was exposed to many provocative images, but I couldn't interpret or reflect any of them. My energy was focused on that empty wine glass and shrinking dope supply.

Today, I realize that art is everywhere. I'm free to be a part of it. I don't have to be high in order to use my imagination.

I can take a photo of the meal I prepare for my family. Do the laundry and hang my clothes neatly in the closet. When I call a friend and spend time catching up on the news… Hey, it's art if I say so!

Art is whatever helps my mind grow and makes my heart feel happy.

Yesterday, I had tons of stuff to do. There'll be even more things that need to get accomplished tomorrow. I am tethered to a busy, productive existence. And in the middle, I have today.

Today is here! And already, I can feel myself rushing it along. Because I like to get things done. I feel safe and satisfied when I can check items off the list in my mind. What's so wrong with that?

Nothing, I guess. But each day is important. And I am right in the center of something nourishing and rejuvenative. The Saturday of my life! This moment has arrived for me to enjoy and appreciate.

I am here, and God is with me. We are together. I say a little prayer that I loosen my grip on what's next and trust God to carry me through.

I've done this before. Everything always works out just fine.

I don't remember much at the very beginning, when I first got clean.

But I do recall wondering about God. And then asking, "Are you there?"

That's when I realized I was waiting for an answer I already had.

Who asks questions into the wind?

From time to time, I make my own trouble. I stick my nose where it doesn't belong. And when someone bites it off, my feelings get hurt.

Not every circumstance requires my involvement. There's a big difference between helping and meddling.

Please help me with this, Lord. Some situations can be slippery.

Sometimes, I bring God these confusing bags of emotional garbage that I just cannot deal with on my own.

"Here you go," I say. "Knock yourself out."

I trust God with all the gruesome details of my heart and mind. Even the darkest, most extreme thoughts that I'm reluctant to admit exist deep within me. Because they make me feel like a monster. Because I don't understand their value, and I'm afraid of all that negativity.

I drag these bundles of crap across the floor and lay them at the Lord's feet unaddressed, in throbbing heaps.

"Be careful," I tell Him. "There's some shit in here that's gonna blow your mind. I'm warning you, it's awful."

"Really, Mary? Is this all you've got?" God asks. "I wish you'd come sooner. It's never as bad as you think."

Perfection is a ridiculous goal. I have never been perfect a day in my life. Why would I assume this moment will be any different?

It's a relief to embrace my flaws as part of what makes me who I am. I'm not always paying attention when folks tell me stuff. I jump to irrational conclusions. I lose my temper with the kids. And good Lord, how I take the world's inventory!

I don't have to like my shortcomings, but I shouldn't beat myself up over them either. Acknowledging that they exist brings me one step closer to making some positive changes.

I can be a work in progress and still enjoy happiness.

I feel like I am becoming a trusted servant, and this means a lot to me.

For the longest time, I could not be counted on for much. I bailed on my responsibilities. I made promises and broke them. I said I'd be somewhere but disappeared instead.

I was strapped to my drinking and drugging, like a dog tied to a fence just beyond the zoo. A double outsider. I barked my fool head off and got all the other animals agitated. I chewed on my leash, not to mention my own foot and tail.

Today, I am learning how to help instead of just showing off. How to be generous without bragging. How to contribute in useful ways. I can do all these things now that I'm sober. Now that I'm free.

The opportunities for growth and development are beyond measure.

I was always looking for something outside of myself to make me happy.

I needed to have a boyfriend in order to feel as though I mattered. I started out with good intentions... or so I thought. But relationships take compromise, and I wanted things my way.

Guys got tired of my bullshit. Fights led to break-ups. I found replacements quickly, so I didn't have to be alone.

Jobs were another problem. I did nice work, but I couldn't get there on time. I was disruptive and unfocused. My bosses grew frustrated with my behavior, and I was fired. Or I just called in sick one day and never went back.

I bought things I couldn't afford and didn't need. I racked up debt and ignored my bills. I had no bank account. I kept whatever money I had in the freezer—cold cash. I joked about it.

I was frantic to fill the void in my life. The strange inexplicable emptiness that was always there and only ever got bigger. I looked to distractions for ways to make me feel complete. I was afraid all the time.

Getting loaded seemed to help. It took the edge off, and the hole shrunk briefly. But when it returned, it came back larger than before. I started falling in. Climbing out became more and more difficult.

When I finally got sober, I experienced moments of real strength for the first time in my life. It was during these pockets of energy that I could be honest with myself. I sat with the uncomfortable feelings that always had me running for the door. I discussed them with folks who cared about my progress.

I allowed God's love and light to shine through those gaps in my heart and heal them. I became whole.

Today, I understand how to create my own joy and satisfaction. Sure, I still get cranky and confused when my expectations aren't met. I'm human. But I don't depend on other people or things to bring me happiness. I take responsibility for the quality of my life.

I keep earning this reward as time goes on. How neat is that?

I don't remember passing through a triumphant arch to freedom. It sounds sensational, but sobriety wasn't like that for me.

It's different for everybody, I suppose. The way we handle situations—or don't. That's how I got myself in such a bind to begin with. I couldn't deal with me.

Nonetheless, I got there. To the sober side. I love being clean. I like being able to understand my feelings and respond in sensible ways. It's fantastic to have a mind that works properly and a body that cooperates with efforts to thrive.

These things are huge, and I am so grateful.

Prayer is like a mini vacation. A brief respite from all the stress and chaos of the day. I can stop right in the middle of whatever I'm doing and get with God immediately. This kind of travel package is all inclusive. No waiting, no hassles, no hidden fees.

I don't have to book reservations, check the weather or bring extra clothes. There's no laundry to contend with when I return. No one even needs to know I'm gone. I can be away for as long as I like and revisit as many times as I please.

Perhaps we'll bump into each other someday. Prayer seems to be a very popular place.

I am worth loving.

I tell myself that this is true. I may not have believed it at first, but I do now.

I am worth loving.

These are gorgeous words. I say them out loud and make them my own.

You really need to try this, even if it feels weird. Just keep at it—until the message sinks in.

I am not the greatest cook. I can put together sandwiches and macaroni from a box. I have trouble following directions and measuring things accurately. I am distracted by fancy spices and complicated gadgets. Some recipes really get the best of me.

It's like this when I have decisions to make. I get flustered. So I bring all the details to God and turn them over, like the contents of a grocery sack. The ingredients can feed my life several different ways. I ask for God's help preparing the meal. I guess this is prayer.

He is a master chef and knows what He's doing in the kitchen.

When I first wake up, I feel anxious. So many questions come to mind.

Logistical details, mostly. What has to get done? Am I ready? Who needs to be where? And when?

I don't like to start my day, buried in apprehension. Running and racing, yet going nowhere.

These questions bring nothing but worry. For crying out loud, I just woke up! I'm still in my pajamas. I have Albert Einstein hair. It's a vulnerable time.

I quietly whisper God's name and invite Him into my thoughts. I want to see things the way God does. That man never looks nervous.

The more time we spend together, the easier it is to recognize His voice. To understand what's important and keep things simple.

Just knowing I'm not alone really helps. Let's deal with today together, Lord.

When I first got sober, rigorous honesty sounded exhausting.

But now that I have strong muscles, it's just a nice workout.

The pills got me up, and the coke hurled me forward. The liquor greased the wheels that kept everything in motion. On my circus train, traveling nowhere.

When I was drinking and doing my thing, I lived like an animal in a cage of my own making. I growled when anyone got too close. I paced back and forth, occasionally sniffing at the lock.

The prospect of freedom from the drugs and the booze was something unfamiliar and scary. I couldn't even try to think it was feasible. I did my tricks, whether I wanted to or not. I kept my paws on either side of my dirty bowl and slept with one eye open.

I preferred when the train was moving. I didn't have to consider what I was missing.

I spent whole days trying to decide who I was gonna hit up for money. Which pigeons would most likely say 'yes' when I tapped them for a loan.

I didn't give a shit what was happening in anyone else's life. I just needed to approach these individuals carefully and separate them from twenty or thirty dollars—so I could keep myself afloat.

These efforts were exhausting. I needed that cash. I considered how these situations would turn out if my lenders refused. The potential for rejection only heightened my delirium.

In my heart, I preferred to borrow rather than rob folks. But realistically, I could do both.

In recovery, these dark shadows become prayers of thanks. It is entirely possible to build and regain trust, but words without deeds are meaningless. Making amends is a rational process that combines feeling with doing. It paves the way to that healing grace.

With God's love, the help of a sponsor and the insight of my sober community of friends, I fumbled through the awkward discomfort of my shameful behavior. When I made that list of all the people I'd shortchanged and let down, I got right to work trying to repair the damage.

Making amends continues to afford me the opportunity to turn my ugliness into a rich, beautiful history and promising future.

Each day reminds me just how precious forgiveness really is.

I can choose to feel good about who I am. Every morning, I remind myself that I have this choice. Options are awesome.

I suppose I can decide to feel like shit if I want to. But why on earth would I do that? It just doesn't make any sense.

When I am trying to understand another person's feelings, I can't help but respond with love. This is an idyllic position for a control freak like myself.

I can put aside my opinions and perceived slights, my history of involvement. I don't have to get weighed down with resentments that go nowhere.

I can just be in that moment of compassion for someone else's situation. I can give that individual the space he or she requires to make decisions. It's not necessary that I dive in and save the day or inadvertently stir up additional trouble.

I can care about what's going on without sticking my nose where it doesn't belong or attempting to impact the outcome.

I can also explore my own feelings from a safe location. Empathy goes a long way toward contributing to the good health of my relationships. And most importantly, it protects my overall serenity.

Old thoughts and feelings are comforting, no matter how screwed up they are. I turn toward them reflexively sometimes, even though they bring me nothing but confusion and drama. I am sentimental for the past. For that pocket of time before everything turned to shit.

Today, I take careful steps in a new direction. I practice behaviors that were foreign to me. I have reliable tools to help me process emotions that used to dump me on my ass. I see God—and shining examples of His light—everywhere I go.

I reach for these valuable resources and create a stable future for myself and my family. I try to share what I know without showing off.

Sobriety does work. It is satisfying and rewarding. I am living proof.

This is a much better way for me to be in the world.

I fought with people all the time when I was getting high. I constantly felt tested and provoked. I obsessed about confrontations I would have. What I was gonna say and how the other person would respond. My clever comebacks and the closing argument that would absolutely seal the deal—proving to the world once and for all—that I was right and everyone else was wrong. I get tired just thinking about it.

I need to remind myself that I am a witless fighter, and I have no business thinking otherwise. I may start out strong but as soon as that initial blast of adrenaline gets shot, I turn to tears. I have nothing to back up my tough talk.

I don't want to fight with anybody. I suck at it.

Today when I feel challenged, I try to step back from the situation and figure out what's really going on and whether or not my participation is even necessary. It's easy to get caught up in someone else's hysteria. Adding my own to the mix never helps.

I used to be proud of just how much I could drink. And snort. And smoke. I'd stay up all night and party. Go to work the next day—no problem. I wanted to feel good about my capacity for getting wasted.

But there were problems. Lots of them.

I neglected my responsibilities. My performance on the job suffered. I pissed away more money than I made. I was careless in my relationships. I routinely played the fool.

I ignored messages that everything was out of whack. Plus, addiction has a way of dimming the lights and turning the music up even louder. So I couldn't see the signs or hear the warnings. And besides, I didn't want any of it to be true.

I was just in the moment, having fun. Living. Right?

I'm amazed at how disillusioned I was. I worked hard to not recognize what was going on. Even when it sat on my chest like a drunken 800-pound gorilla with an insane drug habit. It's nearly impossible to pretend something like that isn't crushing you. But I did.

Today, I put all that effort and energy into my recovery. In 24-hour intervals, I try to concentrate on staying sober, making healthy choices and getting to know myself.

I want to understand why I was so uncomfortable to begin with. Why I had to reach for booze and dope to make even the most harmless situations better. I figure things out a little bit at a time.

I don't have to avoid my life any longer. I want to live it.

"What do you want to talk about, God?"

I pause for half a second and try to imagine the Lord's other interests.

Then I go right back to chewing His ear about myself.

What a precious gift it is to be sober!

To know friendship and truly be a friend. To look in someone else's eyes, to hear their story and see myself reflected back.

Friendship is a warm, soft light in my life.

I love not feeling alone.

I can't save the world. I wish I could. I'd love the credit.

But I'm not God. Sometimes, I forget. It bums me out.

I like big gestures. Broad, sweeping sentiments. I always have. This impractical approach has gotten me into so much trouble.

I am far more productive and successful when I do little things that make me feel like I'm contributing to a larger goodness.

I'm not in charge, but I can help.

Whenever I drank and used, the search was on for a very specific set of perfect conditions—none of which I could guarantee or enjoy with any regularity. I chased these ideal parameters for years and years and years. Like a dog that perks up when the garbage truck passes. It smells something interesting and can't help but take off running after it.

As each experience fell short of the intended outcome, my appetite grew. Until I could no longer control the urge to get high or secure enough supplies to meet that need. Neither of these unreliable factors ever stopped me from trying. I tore open every bag of trash I could sink my teeth into.

I wanted out of my discomfort so badly. Anything was better than where I was. I could not satisfy my hunger with normal emotional responses. I had none. I needed to be high in order to just keep functioning. It became the only thing in my life that made sense.

How crazy. I can't even believe I let it happen.

I swear, I didn't know that's what was going on at the time.

I stared at the door to a better life. For years, I shouted at people on the other side and kicked at it like a child. I pretended it wasn't there, crawling out windows instead or insisting I was trapped. I slumped against the way out and slid to the floor, defeated.

There is no lock on the door to recovery, but I had to come through it on my own. It is the door to a better life. A life I couldn't even begin to imagine when I was using. A life I sometimes feel I don't deserve, but for which I am forever grateful.

I used to get sick all the time.

Common colds kicked my ass. I bruised easily, and cuts wouldn't heal. My face broke out. My teeth were loose and fell apart. Being wrecked was a workout, boy.

Equipment failure is scary. I felt ugly and old. My fears made things worse. I drank and got high to push the problems further into the back of my mind, so I didn't have to think about them.

But my mouth hurt and my head throbbed. The physical stuff was a constant reminder that something was terribly wrong.

Recovery changes everything.

Today, I feel good about my body. I am sturdy and strong. I honor commitments to my health. I have check-ups with my doctor, and I go to the dentist regularly. I am honest about my drug history. I take care of myself, so I can enjoy my life.

I smile often. There's a lot to smile about.

I believe that God is love.

Nobody says you have to. That's your choice.

But if you do, give Him your heart. Let Him have the whole thing. Put it in a safe place as you rediscover yourself.

At 52 years of age, I have only one serious regret.

I wish I hadn't pierced my left earlobe so many times.

I'm good with just about everything else.

Man, did I lean on others—instead of taking care of my obligations. I helped myself to their generosity. I slept on couches, borrowed clothes and mooched rides. I let them make important decisions that I should have been handling on my own.

But when things didn't work out the way I wanted, I always shifted the blame. It wasn't my fault that I missed appointments. Got fired. Let people down.

"Coming here was your idea. Not mine."

"I never wanted that job in the first place."

"Why don't you mind your own business?"

Today, I understand that even if I let someone else do my work, I'm still accountable for what happens. And I'm grateful that I take responsibility for my life. It feels good to stand on my own two feet.

It's also an important reminder when I want to dive in and fix another person's troubling situation. I just can't do it. I can lend an ear and offer encouragement. I can tell them what I did. But the real effort is entirely up to them.

I greet people warmly, even if we're strangers.

I don't lunge at folks or go out of my way to give anyone the creeps. But "Good Morning" isn't gonna kill me.

Most of the time, friendliness abounds! How lovely to be part of such a brief, yet pleasant exchange.

My heart is full. It truly is a wonderful morning.

Sometimes, my thoughts get over-excited. I'm not sure how it happens. I like to say 'yes' to so many things. I don't notice if I'm tired or hungry. And before I know it, I'm completely anxious and unsettled.

My mind becomes a carousel that spins way too quickly. I can almost see the riders being flung from their horses. The music doesn't match the chaos.

I have to step away from the turmoil and take care of myself.

I start with prayer. I may not even have the words to explain what I'm feeling, but I just get with God. Let Him know that I'm going through something.

I listen to the messages my body sends me. Rest and meals are good. I replenish my physical energy so I can think clearly.

Meetings. I refresh my commitment to recovery. I can always bring my concerns to the group, where I trust my thoughts will be considered and respected.

My serenity returns when I focus on these simple adjustments.

Now that I'm making all these improvements in my life, I can't believe how easy it is to appreciate being sober. I want the same beautiful opportunities for the folks I care about.

I have to remember that we change when we're ready. I must allow my friends and family to be themselves. I can't force my way of thinking on others.

I certainly didn't like it when people tried to pull that shit with me. They could shove their advice and suggestions straight up their own asses. I didn't need any help.

Yeah, I remember how that went.

The best thing I can do is continue to work on myself. Provide a sturdy example of what it means to grow and heal. I can leave the door open—in case anyone wants to join me.

Despite the challenges that present themselves in my life, there is always something to be thankful for. I try to nurture my relationship with gratitude first thing in the morning. Before my feet hit the floor and the world starts breaking my balls.

You see what I mean? I was peaceful and receptive just a minute ago. Minding my own business, laying the spiritual groundwork for the rest of my day. I must have let some other feeling push my appreciation aside. Probably cynicism or self-pity. Those guys get up so early! And they have big muscles.

I can bring my gratitude back through practice. Celebrating simple joys and subtle advantages is an effective habit. I try to focus on these gifts and blessings. There's far too many to count. I guess that's why I don't ever count them.

I start with the smell of coffee and having an oversized cup to drink it from. The presence of my children relaxing in my bed, quarreling over something so stupid—I could totally kick them both from where I'm sitting.

Well, that was quick. And here we go again.

It's okay, really. I just keep trying. I am a work in progress.

The people I've met in recovery have always helped me appreciate that I'm right where I need to be.

It's reassuring that no matter where I am, there's someplace I belong.

I can bring that feeling everywhere I go.

I am okay, no matter what. Even if things don't go the way I've planned. When a situation throws me a curve that I wasn't expecting, and I lose my balance. When someone treats me unkindly. When I feel overwhelmed.

I remind myself that I'm okay. I repeat these words as many times as necessary, until I believe them.

Today is so brief, when I really think about it. Twenty-four hours is not that long. The world is always changing and becoming something different.

I can pray and remember that God is on board for the ride. Together we can move through whatever it is that's freaking me out and making me nuts. I can handle transient moments of upsetment. They suck, but they're not gonna kill me. And they don't last forever.

I can deal with disappointment and move forward with a clear head and a steady heart. I can get myself to that place of peacefulness that I've come to really appreciate, without the use of drugs or the help of a drink to ease the discomfort.

I am okay, no matter what.

I am an alcoholic and a drug addict. I cannot afford to dick around with the truth.

There's no reason for me to cut through the beer aisle at the grocery store. Or order food cooked in brandy at a restaurant, simply because I'm dressed up. I don't need champagne flutes or shot glasses stored in a cabinet over the kitchen sink, just in case. It's bad enough that empty wine rack built into the wall mocks me.

I shouldn't wear shirts that say "Screw work. Let's party!" or watch films that promote getting high. I can't be lax in my casual conversations about such pastimes.

Getting myself into bed at a reasonable hour is a great policy. The night's not supposed to last forever. It isn't necessary that I know where my husband keeps the Tylenol PMs. I should also respect the alarm clock in the morning. That snooze button is more trouble than it's worth.

I have to be thoroughly honest for recovery to work. Otherwise, all that anguish that brought me to my knees will be back again to kick me squarely in the teeth.

I didn't mean to hurt you. It wasn't my intention. Still, I know I did.

I'm sorry I was secretive. I lied to try and cover things up. So I wouldn't get caught. Plus, I was afraid if you found out, you wouldn't love me anymore.

You'd want me to stop. And I didn't think I could.

There were so many excuses to keep doing what I was doing. At the time, they felt like reasons. But they just weren't.

I understand the difference now.

I have adopted an attitude of positive thinking in everything I do. That doesn't mean I'm a nut job.

It's just that I've come to realize when I allow my mind to think negatively, I'm not doing myself any big favors.

God gives me exactly what I need.

But sometimes, I want more. And then when I get it, I panic and feel anxious. I start to doubt myself. I think perhaps I will not be able to accomplish whatever it is that one part of me suggests I can do while another part says, "You must be joking."

So I go back to God, apprehensive and stressed out.

"It's too much," I tell Him. "You're gonna have to help me."

And of course, He does. He already is. Like always.

I try to remember that God's in charge, and He only gives me what I can handle. He's made arrangements so that I can know Him and experience unbelievable changes in my life. He blesses me in ways that I don't understand but probably shouldn't challenge.

I really just need to be cool and let God do His job.

I am in this moment that will be over by the time I finish this sentence.

How temporary is that?

Dig this…

I watch what I eat. I take vitamins. I make sure to get enough rest. I am living a healthy lifestyle. On top of that, I have become a spiritual being.

When I think about it, I crack myself up. My life wasn't anything like this. And if you told me that it could be, I'd have thought you were half crazy.

Sometimes, I can't decide if this transformation is truly a miracle or just plain hilarious. I guess it all depends on what kind of mood I'm in.

Mostly, I'll go with miracle. It's not as funny as it is excellent.

I thank God for my useless years. I really do.

Each memory has become a valuable asset.

In sharing the worst, I can hope for the best.

If I ignore where I came from, I may forget what I've done. If I forget what I've done, I may do it again. And if I do it again, I'm right back where I started.

This doesn't mean I get to wallow in the past. But remembering is a really good idea.

My contribution to the universe is important. But I'm not exactly sure what my skills and talents are.

Everyone else seems to know what they're doing. Most of the time, I feel like I'm hanging on by the seat of my pants.

Why am I even here? What does it really matter?

These are big questions. Too big for answers that make any sense as I slide my feet out of bed and onto the floor for one more day, sober and present.

I look in the mirror and recognize my face in the reflection. I may not always be pleased with what I see, but what I see is real. This is significant.

I've been given a chance to begin again. I don't want to waste it, stuck in neutral.

It's time to wake up and find out how I can make the world a better place.

Yikes! I will start with this hair.

I didn't know how to talk to God. In the beginning, He was just another person who couldn't understand what I was going through.

I hated that awkward part at the end of the meeting. Where everybody held hands and prayed The Our Father. My lips moving to the words I recognized by heart but didn't understand and hadn't said for so long. I felt like a phony. Besides, I didn't know any of these strangers.

I'd turned away from God and was reluctant to let Him back into my life. What was left of it. If I was gonna get sober, I wanted to do it on my own. The fewer people involved in my embarrassment, the better. That's how I felt.

Nonetheless at every angle, there was God. Just hanging out, waiting for me to feel less uneasy with His presence. I started seeing Him in the faces of the men and women I met in my recovery. He existed in every story of frustration and redemption that was shared.

I remembered our relationship. I wanted Him with me again, in a new and healthy way. I prayed, and there He was. He was always there. And still is. God has seen it all.

Today at meetings when we say The Lord's Prayer, I feel privileged to stand in that circle of unity, among friends with whom I share similar challenges and goals.

I welcome God's guidance and strength. I am a channel of His continuous love.

Plus, I really dig the cheer at the end. The part that goes, "Keep coming back. It works if you work it. So work it, you're worth it!" I used to think it was corny. But now, I just love it. Because it's true.

Knowing what I know about myself and what I've learned along the way, I always hope my children will have an easier time figuring out who they are.

If they don't, I pray that eventually they will. It's completely up to them. The same as it is for me.

I can't do heavy thinking all day long. It would be like a gym class that never ends.

Sometimes, my brain just needs a little break.

Let's sit on the bleachers for a few minutes. We can talk about boys and music.

I needed to let go of my old self if my life was to truly change. But I was surrounded by and involved with so many people. How could I just disconnect like that?

Not every relationship would survive this incredible upheaval. What a terrifying thought.

I wanted to believe that sobriety was the right decision. I also wanted everyone to embrace and accept the New Me. I couldn't imagine losing any of my family or friends. This kind of expectation is impractical and potentially disastrous.

Not everyone comes back when recovery occurs. They're really not supposed to. In the best interest of my on-going good health, certain individuals cannot exist in my life. They must become a part of my past.

We're all making decisions as far as what we need. One of the important things I've come to understand is that I can still love some folks, but I may never see them again.

When a friend pays me a compliment and I don't agree, I still say 'thank you.' I am grateful.

He or she recognizes something in me that I don't see in myself.

It's not enough for me to just occasionally remember that God exists. That He's out there somewhere, floating around. Doing whatever. I want in on the action. Every minute of every day, I like to know that I'm God's favorite. So are you, but I'm not threatened. As a matter of fact, I think it's terrific.

There is no shame in my spiritual game. When I pray, I feel great. My efforts remind me that God is alive in my heart, and He's psyched that I want to be near Him. He sees me drag my chair closer to His presence, and He can't help but smile. He recognizes all the progress I am making. I feel His hand on my shoulder, and I love it.

I make time for God because He is where everything fabulous comes from. Faith transforms my life into a groovy celebration.

I am powerless over alcohol. It's the truth. The same goes for cocaine and amphetamines. I love them like nothing else, and there will never be enough to fill the crater inside of me that always says 'go.'

I wonder about that hole sometimes, and why I am so different. Why I can't just prep one line and get tight. Or have two drinks with friends before heading home. Maybe smoke a joint to relax. How come other folks can party on the weekends and get back to their lives and jobs without issue?

I can't. I will never be able to. When drugs and booze are involved, I have no discretion. The shit makes me crazy. I admit it. I am defeated.

I pray about these thoughts that I have. I ask God why He made me this way, with the potential for such recklessness. In each sober moment, He helps me realize these challenges are shaping my character as I travel on this road of self-discovery.

I am free of the chains that bound me to the endless grind. I'm filling the vacuous expanse with positive energy. Rebuilding my life a day at a time. I can identify my feelings now without getting spooked. I put my head on the pillow at night and pretty much go right to sleep. I wake up well rested.

Being powerless doesn't mean I'm weak. It means I'm smart. And aware. What a magnificent revelation.

I never know what a new friend will look like.

All I know is how good it feels to have one.

No matter how much sober time I cobble together, the miracle happens only one way. A day at a time.

The rules never change. The steps remain simple.

And thank God. Because I do tend to over-complicate things.

I can't have just one drink. Or two. Or seven. That's not how things work for me.

The first sip is the one that gets me plastered. The one that will convince me to drive drunk, drain my bank account, buy cocaine and speed. Leave my young children unsupervised.

That initial taste will have me lying through my teeth to the people I love and clearing my calendar to get more. Keep going.

I need to acknowledge and respect this simple fact of my life. Because there's always so much at stake.

Letting go seems like a backward way to approach progress.

I am crisis-driven. I want action and results, and I want them now! When the potential for argument presents itself, everything inside of me screams "DO SOMETHING!"

Letting go is such a powerful affirmation. It requires discipline and self-control. It helps me release my anger toward the person with whom I'm unhappy without engaging in conflict. I can put aside my negative feelings and allow myself to be peaceful almost immediately. I don't have to try and prove my point—you know, just so I can see how it goes. C'mon, it never goes well.

I am free to walk away from any situation where someone could get hurt. I'm not making anything better with a fight. The problems just continue and invariably get worse, with me tangled up in the turmoil.

When I let go, I can forgive myself for any association with what's already occurred. I can invite myself to forgive others. I can't change the past, but I can focus on what's ahead.

Recently, I came across some pictures of myself when I was using. It was clear that I was drunk and scorched on whatever. I was in my pajamas, looking gaunt and half insane.

I don't like these photos. But for some reason, I won't throw them away. I stare into the crazy version of my own face, searching for myself. Wondering where I went during all that time away.

I am drawn to these images of yesterday. It's not as though I want to go back and linger. Perhaps only to grab myself by the shoulders and yank me out of there. But knowing myself as I do, I would never go. I'd curl my hands up near my chest and pull my body into a ball.

"Just let me be," I'd insist. "I'm fine."

Last night, my husband mentioned this one particular phrase that always worried him like nothing else.

"You used to say, 'I'll figure something out.' I wasn't sure what that was supposed to mean," he said.

"It probably just meant, 'Leave me alone.'"

He smiled, uneasily. "I bet you're right."

Happiness is my decision.

If something in my life is making me unhappy, I can always change it. If I don't, no one else will. It's not their job.

If another person is influencing my mood negatively, the only thing I can do is adjust my life accordingly. Their behavior is their responsibility, as is mine.

These days, whenever I get confused, I try to figure out if there's anything I should be doing or anything that actually needs to be done. Now I know that these two approaches can be completely different.

I've yet to receive any factory recall notices for those parts of my brain that give me trouble.

That being said, I really just need to do the very best I can with the original equipment I've been issued.

I accept all of me, exactly as I am.

Oh, my God. Who am I kidding? No, I don't. I want to, but I just can't do it all the time. I'd be a liar if I said I could.

So, you know what? Scratch that. Let's try a different approach.

I'd like to accept all of me, exactly as I am.

That's much better. At least it's honest. I will start from this position instead.

Thank you, God.

How great it is to be given a reprieve from diving head first into full-blown crazy.

Lord, I have a brilliant idea. Let's hang out together all day! I love your company.

Of course, there's lots of stuff that needs to get done—like always. Household chores and errands. Plus, I promised the boys I'd take them to the gym and then, the pool. Out to dinner, if they don't bust my chops. The schedule keeps filling up, even as we speak.

But I know you enjoy the gift of my time. No matter how frenzied things get.

You can watch me in action. You do that anyway.

How about we just say I thought of it first?

Sobriety doesn't happen overnight. Wouldn't that be phenomenal?

"You know, I've been thinking. I am so done with this bullshit. Starting tomorrow, no more booze for me. As a matter of fact, I'm gonna flush this dope down the toilet, brush my teeth and go to bed. See you in the morning!"

And just like that, problem solved. Next day, you arise with an unburdened heart. You feel connected to the world. Both mind and body, free of compulsion. Forever.

Wake up. You're having a dream.

Making the decision to give up drugs and alcohol is only the beginning of a thrilling journey toward an amazing life. It's like moving to another planet. There's excitement and intrigue, space travel, Tang. Plus tons of miscellaneous details that need to be ironed out while you're floating around beyond the earth's atmosphere.

I wish I knew exactly how long it takes for a person to truly get sober. Then, I could just say to those who are struggling, "Don't worry. Everything will be cool in a month and a half."

I think I started feeling better at around the six-week mark, but only physically. Parts of me were raring to go . But emotionally, I was still a wreck. Everybody's parts are different.

I guess that's why it's so important to keep coming back to meetings. We can share and listen to one another. Discuss smart ways to transfer all this on-the-job training into real world experience.

I'd love for us to be together in that moment when recovery starts making sense for you. When you realize you're actually learning how to live and live well. And you start understanding what everybody's so excited about.

I hope you'll sit with me.

I tell myself I am at peace, especially when I feel restless.
"Damn it. I am at peace!"

By saying the words, however ludicrous, I am clearing a
mental path. I bring my mind a little closer to that soothing
place, where I can be calm in my heart.

"I am at peace."

I am not the relaxing type. I need to practice doing this
thing that does not come naturally. Until I get as close as I
can to what I think I should be feeling. Some kind of gentle
relief, I guess. That sounds nice.

I turn my discomfort into a devotion. I want the Lord to
know I am trying. With God by my side, I have faith I will
arrive when the time is right.

And until then, I just keep praying that I stay cool.

I miss getting high. No, wait. I miss the perfect version of getting high, which happened so infrequently, compared to the nightmare of what ordinarily went down. It's a joke to suggest otherwise.

But a part of me still wishes things were different. They're not. This is how I am, and here's how it is.

I remind myself that I don't want to find out what picking up again will feel like. I already know it won't be good. And it'll be far worse than before because I will have let it happen. If I go back out, it will surely kill me. It wants me dead anyway. I may not even care at that point.

At least this way, I get to have a chance at a decent life. I can experience opportunities I wouldn't even give a damn about if I was loaded.

My thoughts are free and clear. Yes, some of them are uncomfortable. But at least they're real thoughts and not merely urges. That's for animals. I want to be done behaving like an animal.

I can still have lots of things. I just can't get high anymore.

Just because I'm whatever age I am doesn't mean anything. This detail is irrelevant.

I can't go back and change anything or get hung up on all that time I spent spinning my wheels. I remember staring into the mirror when I was 37 years old, behaving like a child but feeling ancient.

I'm here right now. I'm present, and I'm sober. That's a pretty big deal.

I used to worry about heart attacks. That I was gonna have one in the middle of the night while my husband slept. That he'd wake up and find me dead, with my drugs and a glass of wine nearby. Empty bottles hidden all over the house.

I thought about how sad he'd be. A grown man, crying like that. Tricked into thinking I was a good choice, then realizing he was wrong.

That's no way to live, always worrying about getting caught. Wondering whether an awful accident is about to happen. It's just torment for everyone involved.

I'm overjoyed to be clean. I feel ready for whatever's next.

I try not to beg God for what I want. When I keep asking for the same thing over and over, I demonstrate a lack of faith in His ability to answer my prayers.

I know the Lord never gets insulted.

But it'd be nice if I gave the guy a break every once in a while.

Forward and back, forward and back. This is the path to my recovery. The road is seldom smooth, and movement seems both fast and slow.

Sometimes, it feels like I'm standing still. Even the birds come to rest. They perch on my heavy shoulders. They think I am a statue.

"C'mon, you guys. "Cut me some slack," I say.

I shake them loose. They flap their wings and fly off into the sky. I want to follow them. To feel something. Anything.

I watch for a minute and realize that I am moving. Changes are happening. I just don't always notice them.

Healing takes place as I walk along this road. To a better me.

My children have their own lives to live, but they are watching and listening to mine. I am influencing their thoughts and actions with the way I behave. Through my example, they are developing an awareness of how the world works.

The way I respond to folks I encounter during the course of my day. How I speak to my husband and friends. When I drop the ball on a commitment or treat someone rudely, my kids are taking notes.

And guaranteed, they will refer to this information as readily as they will the good things I do.

I am human. I am not perfect. I make mistakes. And when I do, I get upset.

I feel guilty. Because I'm human. And not perfect. I realize how dumb this sounds.

Nonetheless, I am embarrassed when I screw something up. I hold onto the shame as if it were some kind of punishment that I must endure.

Perhaps I'm not ready to take responsibility for my actions. Or I don't want to admit that I need to start over from the beginning. These are excuses that keep me stuck in my discomfort.

Forgiveness is the only real way to change the situation. If I don't, I'll just keep going round and round. Feeling regretful and unhappy. Unable to move forward.

I need to remind myself that I can't be right all the time. I have to be wrong in order for things to even out. Otherwise, I'll never appreciate the difference.

And then, I wouldn't be human. And I most certainly wouldn't be me.

I thought my friends were triggers—because all I did whenever we got together was get fucked up. So many adventures and all that crazy antics. These details had become such a big part of who I was. And suddenly, they were taken completely off the table.

It wasn't my friends' fault. None of them drank like me or had to keep the party going for three days. They wanted to do other things. Have coffee and go shopping, maybe see a movie. I wasn't interested if I couldn't get loaded. So I gave them excuses or didn't show up when we were supposed to meet.

Once I got sober, it took a while to figure that one out. These relationships weren't unhealthy—I was. I felt afraid and embarrassed. Confused about what really went on. These folks had always been good to me, and I treated them poorly. I realized why I'd chosen these friends to begin with. Because they were good.

I see the present with new eyes. How rare it is to be given this kind of second chance.

When I am in need of a shower, all the hand-washing in the world isn't gonna help me feel clean. I have to get rid of my stinky clothes and just be in the water. Use soap and shampoo on my skin and hair. Expose every surface to a rigorous scrubbing and simply start over.

When I am done, I feel invigorated. I'm no longer preoccupied with my own nastiness. I get some deodorant happening and brush my teeth. A fresh shirt and pants. I can focus on other things that require my attention.

There are no shortcuts to good hygiene. Sobriety is the same way. I have to strip down to the basics and be vulnerable in order to get anything significant accomplished.

I wish I could figure out exactly what God is trying to teach me. The lessons He wants me to learn. Sometimes, they feel so vague.

Maybe if I knew just a little bit about the challenges that He has in store, I'd be more cooperative. At least, I would know what to wear.

I realize how ridiculous this request is. Of course, I'd still resist. Perhaps twice as much. The details might paralyze me with fear.

I just need to remember that everything is going to be okay. I trust God with my life. My doubts are what keep me honest.

I wake up to another new day. I say my prayers and sit in quiet reflection for a few minutes. I wonder who I really am. I want specific answers to questions I don't even know how to ask.

I'm getting more familiar with myself as time goes on. Nonetheless, it would be nice if all this progress could be explained more clearly. Especially when I feel willful and distracted, still wanting things I cannot have.

I bring my mind back around to right now. I focus on my blessings. I remind myself that everything is good. And everything will be just fine.

I have a sober me, and that's a great position from which to move forward.

In the made-for-TV movie about my life, I think it should start out in black and white. Then go to Technicolor once I get sober.

Kind of like in *The Wizard of Oz*, only a little more gradual. With a contemporary soundtrack.

I wanted my drinking to lead me into those smooth, glossy moments—where I felt relaxed and confident. Popular, desirable and worthy of a good time. Where my mind was at ease, and my fears dissolved.

Here's to that ultimate delusion of grandeur, in the face of startling evidence to the contrary. The false hope I clung to, reassuring me that everyone drank. That I was in control. My titanic capacity for alcohol was a virtue! I could stop whenever I wanted. And the most absurd misconception of all, that nobody knew what I was doing.

I wanted all my concerns and worries to be taken care of. So I could just drink in peace. But what I wanted and what I got were never the same thing.

If left to my own devices, if my head and heart aren't working together to make smart choices, I can screw shit up in a hot minute. Less time than that, even. Seconds. The moment I decide I've got everything under control and nobody needs to butt in, I'm headed for trouble.

I might be angry. Or tired. I may be too closely attached to what's going on to see things from a practical perspective. Perhaps I'm hoping for a particular outcome and feel incapable of allowing any wiggle room.

I don't always know the right thing to do. My ability to make sound decisions can be inconsistent. It's getting better, but I wouldn't exactly call it a reflex.

Enter safe people with which to discuss possibilities and alternatives. Folks who have my best interest at heart. Friends who value my happiness but are willing to tell me the truth. Other humans with whom I share this planet. I do not live in a vacuum.

It's not necessary that I charge into battle with my pants around my ankles. I can always borrow gear from the other soldiers. Protecting myself is important.

Besides, not every situation is a war. I might not even have to fight. I can talk things over in the bunker with my comrades. I can climb out of the hole and just go home if I want.

I generally don't recognize this option on my own, and it saves my ass routinely.

Civilized discussions are crucial to my well-being. They get me outside of my own head. I'd be making a lot more mistakes without them.

In the beginning, the Steps seemed inconceivable.

Somebody in a meeting asked me to read them out loud, and my eyes bounced all over the page. Folks referred to them by number, and others nodded their heads. I couldn't memorize a damn thing.

In the back of this book I was given, there they were again. I made a copy and stuffed it in my purse. I slipped another under my pillow. I kept looking at those instructions. I really liked how they were in a list, all neat and orderly.

As the days added up, I got more familiar with the first three. The ones about God, I felt I could at least try. I wanted comfort. But to hell with the rest. Five, eight and nine, especially. They weren't happening. Sharing my embarrassment? Saying I'm sorry? Making things right? I didn't know how.

I just took a glance at the Steps a minute ago when I was praying. I've done them all, even the hard ones. I like to go back over them regularly because they are a good review.

Why not? I keep making mistakes. But I handle my shortcomings differently now than when I was drinking and using.

I love the Steps. For me, they provide a necessary guideline for living. They helped me crawl and then walk toward something astounding.

I got drunk because I didn't want to be lonely. I couldn't see how all the loneliness came about from my getting drunk.

Thank you, God, for helping me grasp that 'chicken and the egg' concept. Scientific principles, like evolution and gravity, have always made my eyes cross.

Communication is key to my sobriety.

If I stay inside my bustling mind trying to work out all my issues, I will surely eat myself alive. Even in my head, I tend to pull together all the tasks I didn't quite finish yesterday and pile them high on top of the ones I haven't gotten to yet. Just to ensure that I'm overwhelmed.

There isn't enough nutritional value in what I know about problem-solving to sustain a healthy existence. I may resort to my old ways of thinking, and that could be dangerous.

I need exposure to other human beings, reminding me that everyone faces hectic schedules, challenges and disappointments. I'm not that fragile in my bubble of uniqueness. Busy is not always better. Sometimes, taking a little break helps cool my anxiety. And realizing that folks are rooting for me can make all the difference in the world.

I have found that alcoholics and addicts in recovery are some of the smartest, most resourceful, compassionate people on earth. I am fortunate and privileged to call these courageous individuals my friends.

Together, we can help each other stay sober and do good things.

I wanted people to stop talking about me, even if they weren't.

Sometimes, I reminded them. Just for the attention.

I did not want to wait for anything. Fuck the rules.

I got high at the job. I drank in the car. I paid for my dope with other people's money. Nobody was gonna tell me I couldn't do shit.

The same thing happened when I was done getting loaded. I wanted to be fixed right away. Yeah, I went to the meetings. But the whole time, I kept trying to determine how to gather up all the necessary information and just split. Figure things out on my own.

These people don't know me, I thought. *I'll decide what I need.*

That's not how this program works. Recovery is a deliberate intimacy that takes time to develop. All the understanding, connectedness and spirituality—it grows as I do. I stay well in the company of my fellows.

I don't have to feel afraid there won't be enough to go around. They're never gonna run out of hope at meetings. That's one of the reasons I keep coming back.

I like folks to know that I am solid, and I can be depended on. I do what I say I'm gonna do. I steer clear of making outlandish promises. I don't want to bring worry to anyone I care about, ever again.

It used to be that whenever the phone rang, I was on the other end of the line—launching the drama. Hysterical tears and far-fetched tales of woe were my contributions to every situation. It was almost as if I felt like I'd be a disappointment without a jaw-dropping story to tell. I wanted all the attention.

When I am tempted to do something that may jeopardize my sobriety, I think about my relationships and how much they mean to me. How troubling it would be to unleash this kind of crazy behavior on the good people God has brought into my life.

I never dreamed I could be reliable. I thought I was too far gone, and no one would ever trust me again. But here I am. Things are very different. Better. Incredible.

Today, I prefer to be part of the solution, not the problem. This is one of the wondrous gifts of recovery.

I tell myself that I know exactly what I need with regard to feeling satisfied in relationships. This may or may not always be the case, but it is a grand initiative.

I try to be specific about what I will and won't tolerate. Honesty is important to me, and I thrive in a consistent setting. I like friendliness. I keep my requirements simple so I don't have that much to remember when I get overwhelmed.

In moments of weakness or confusion, I might be tempted to play the victim. But I've learned to catch myself. I try to examine how I may have allowed this to happen. Somewhere along the way, I must have ignored my own needs. Being negligent doesn't give me the right to complain because I let people crap all over me.

Close scrutiny of my involvement in situations reminds me that I'm in charge of my life. If I'm uncomfortable, I have to promptly take action. Not wait around until someone shoves my feelings up my ass, and then cry about how much it hurts.

I speak kindly to myself. I know in my heart that I'm doing the best I can. Sure, I make crummy choices every once in a while, but they don't define who I am.

I still think I'm pretty swell.

I no longer want to be normal. I'd rather just be myself.

Tying a load on helped me go somewhere else. It got me outside of my own thoughts and took me to places where responsibility wasn't a priority.

That's not an option anymore. It's crucial that I find ways to cope with moments where I have the urge to escape from whatever it is that's got me feeling all squirrelly.

I can't control the whole universe. I share this place with lots of other people. I realize space is limited. It's unreasonable to not be affected by a wide variety of attitudes and points of view.

When I am responsible, I give myself a chance to think more clearly about what's going on. Recognizing this keeps me present and accountable. I can guide my own thoughts and behavior. Not everything has to be a reaction to what someone else has done.

Once I start worrying about what other folks say and do, I'm projecting into the future. If I feel sorry for myself because of something that's already happened, I am stuck in the past.

It's important that I try and focus on right now. I can deal with my emotions and push through those upsetting moments. I want to stay connected to myself and maximize my sense of calm. So I don't bolt and do something I'll regret.

Thoughts wait their turn for my brain to summon them. That's how it works in my mind. Only one idea at a time.

I remember when thoughts involving drugs and alcohol had such big muscles and superhuman strength. They kept punching all the other thoughts in the face and pushing them to the ground. They held their positions at the front of the line.

My brain kept doing its job, attending to issues and performing to the best of its ability. What did it know? It's just a piece of equipment.

Perhaps it was my heart that started bitching. Grumbling about the unfairness and boredom of such a monotonous existence. And the rest of my body, coming undone. Tired of getting shoved around. Sick all the time.

I'm not sure how the metamorphosis occurred. How a notion of hope squeezed its way through those massive legs of addiction. It must have crawled through a tiny gap, carved by faith, when nobody was looking. And made its way to the administrative office of my brain, whispering an urgent request. I like to think so.

However the change got in, it started a fire that lit up the curtains and turned on the sprinklers. The riffraff scattered just long enough for a few big changes to get made.

Emotional upgrades and safety regulations were put into place. I've got big dudes working the door now.

This is one of the fun ways I explain the miracle of recovery to myself. You should see it inside my head. It's a lively factory of efficiency now.

I accept myself as I am. So not perfect.

I come to God's table with a mixed bag of attributes and flaws. He highlights my potential and gives me cool assignments. Sometimes, I'm a servant and occasionally, a soldier—which, I will admit, I do enjoy.

I like being a badass of goodness.

I am safe and well, and blessed with this life I have.

Yeah, I know. But I really need this, and I want that very badly. Plus, if I only I had these other things, I'd be able to do so much more.

I am safe and well, and blessed with this life I have.

Yes, I get what you're saying. But I can't believe she talked to me that way and treated me so unfairly. Why can't he understand how I feel? And how come they won't do what I ask?

I am safe and well, and blessed with this life I have.

All right already. I hear you. But I really wish I could change this one specific detail that I know will make everything so much better. And if only I could convince her to see things from my perspective. And also get him to try harder.

Ahem. Still safe and well over here. And blessed with this life. Remember?

Fine. I get the point.

I am fortunate. There are reasons why I'm safe and well. I try to focus on the good things that are mine to appreciate. But some days, it's tough.

Keeping it simple can be such hard work. But the benefits are unmatched.

In the beginning, I was still a kid. What did I know? I grew up around drinking. Everybody tied one on. And as I got older, I surrounded myself with people who knew how to get loaded. I loved the environment. I wanted to have a good time, and booze was fun.

Drugs were simply the natural progression of events. They blew my mind open in such a way that customized the whole experience for me. The combination of these two ingredients became my "thing." What I did and who I wanted to be. It felt like an identity. I thought I was becoming someone. And she was smart, attractive and entertaining.

Fast forward years and years. It wasn't anything like that when the wheels finally fell off. Picture me, shuffling among several different liquor stores so no one would suspect I drank too much. Hiding bottles all over the house and forgetting where I'd stashed them. Constantly replacing the wine and beer from the fridge and carting the empties away in secret.

That's how it all ended. Rather unceremoniously. I was agitated. And wishing my husband would go to sleep and stay that way. So I could do my dope in peace. Crawling up into my head with the same troubled thoughts I never actually addressed because I couldn't get a foothold. I stared into space. I drooled. I put so much shit inside my body until I ran out and had to go get more. Some party.

I try not to think all that time wasted was a rip-off. I learned alot. Lessons I couldn't possibly have grasped any other way. It sounds ironic, and I guess it is. I feel grateful and relieved to be out. I realize not everybody's as lucky as me.

I respect my memories and keep them close. I don't ever want to go back there again, and I know I don't have to. I thank God for my recovery. For the tools that hang loosely from a belt around my brain and the folks I've met who help me remember what's important.

Every day feels new because I work a strong program. I work it like a motherfucker. I'm worth it.

I have an awesome purpose today. I don't need to know exactly what it looks like.

Too tight a hold on my plans will lead to disappointment. As long as my heart's in the right place and I make sound choices, everything will be just fine.

I look forward to whatever experiences God brings my way.

I'm just a massive control freak, doing my best to be flexible.

I don't know everything.
I will never know everything.
I will make mistakes.
That's reality.

I can learn stuff.
I can develop skills.
I can make decisions based on the knowledge I acquire.
That's progress.

I am clean. I am sober.
For the most part, I am peaceful.
I am intellectually available and emotionally present.
That's a miracle.

I ask the Lord for a smooth heart. Mine gets banged up on a regular basis. I'm rough on my equipment, and God has a way of making all things new.

When I lose my focus, I can always begin again. Every day. Every hour, if I need to. Every minute, even. There's no rule that says I can't.

Starting over is a great feeling.

Sometimes, things tip out of control. The smallest, most insignificant details have a way of throwing my life completely off balance. It's not the end of the world. But good Lord, it certainly feels like it.

My addictive nature preys on me when I am vulnerable. It's always hoping I slide back into the way I used to deal with my obligations—the ridiculous Run and Hide method. I try to be careful when I feel myself getting anxious. It doesn't matter how much clean time I have. Some situations are just dangerous, and I need to be vigilant.

Whenever I feel stressed out, I stop and pray. Even if I've convinced myself I'm on fire. Clearly, I'm not, if I'm having this conversation with God.

Prayer diffuses stressful emotions for me. It helps me realize that everything is still gonna be there in two minutes, five minutes, half an hour. Just enough time to recognize that the Lord wants to help me carry the burden, and that He's super strong.

So I pray and share my crazy head with God. The load gets lighter, and I don't feel so alone. It's easier to decide exactly what needs to get done. I start there.

I remember feeling sorry for myself because of all the shit that happened to me as a kid. Because my mother was strict and my dad wasn't around. My bosses were mean. I started to feel sorry for myself because of all the boyfriends who did me wrong over the years. I felt sorry for myself because the world was out to get me. And just in case I overlooked anyone, I made certain to feel sorry for myself because I had so much to be sorry about.

None of this energy got anything accomplished. But it sure was exhausting.

Today, I don't need to behave this way. I don't have to blame other people so I can feel better about what's going on. That isn't fair. I'm taking responsibility for my actions and getting things done. I can own my feelings, even when they suck. And share what I know, with the hope that something catches on in a good way.

This is my recovery, and it's the most important thing in my life. More important than love, success, my kids. It has to be. Because without it, I've got nothing.

I am mostly governed by fear. I scare easily.

That's why I drank and used. It made me feel bold, sexy and confident. But I was just pretending. I wasn't any of those things in real life. I had no real life. It was all an act.

I don't want to be afraid, but I am human. And now, I live each day without the drink and my dope to lean on. I am exposed all the time.

Therefore, I put my trust in God. He is my source of strength. God can do everything. Period. In His awesomeness, He is able to fill me with the courage I need to be myself in the world. And truly believe that I'm something worth sharing.

He aligns me with good people. I can't do any of this on my own. I need the help of others like me. Folks who understand exactly what this feels like. I value my recovery community.

Together and independently, we can be free.

I was going nowhere, but it felt like movement. All the plotting, deception and subterfuge. Busy, busy, busy. I thought for sure I knew the way.

Every day, I lifted my drink and divvied up my drugs. I didn't ask for directions. I just went. I had no idea where I wanted to be or how to get there.

I spun around and around in a circle, digging a hole. Going down.

Today is different and better. Today, my mind is clear and my body is strong. I have a map in my hand, a little money in my pocket and trustworthy companions by my side.

Sobriety is a thrilling adventure.

I didn't want to pray.
I didn't want to say I was sorry.
I didn't want to have to sit through meetings.
I didn't want to give up the comfort of my misery.

I tried to think of ways I could get around going without.
I really just wanted to keep my body from turning on me.
Plus, I loved how it felt. Getting loaded was my favorite.

My bottom remains vague.
I didn't realize it was a turning point.
I can see it now, but not then.
I don't know what changed the day hope got in and helped
me put my shit down. I can only think it was God, lifting
the burden from my shoulders.

I've found what works for me.
Prayer and honest reflection. Incorporating the Steps into
my everyday life. Food and sleep.
Sharing what I know and keeping what I have.
Whatever this is called, I'm all in.
I never want to go back to how it was.

Hearing other people share their stories makes my story less shameful. Listening when they discuss their feelings makes my feelings more accessible. Being willing to learn from every experience makes my experiences more worthwhile.

God equips me with so many resources. Appreciating His endless love fills me with a strength I didn't know I had.

Guilt is a crippling emotion. It hangs around the periphery of my questionable decisions, latching onto my self-esteem and compromising all growth and development. Guilt shuts my progress down like nothing else. It's a silent killer.

That's why it's important for me to be truthful, so I don't get confused. When I do something wrong, I need to take responsibility for my actions right away. Be specific in my amends. I can learn from these mistakes and move forward with a clear conscience.

By doing this, I keep guilt from festering in pockets of insecurity. I am free to enjoy my own happiness and get back to having fun.

I open the door and let the power of love and virtue enter my life. It arrives in different forms and faces. I never know what these things might look like, so it's important that I'm observant and available.

My problems are a custom fit. They're in my life to teach me things about myself. Obstacles help me become a stronger person. Setbacks encourage me to flex muscles I didn't know I had. Disappointments provide the opportunity to re-establish my priorities.

That doesn't mean I'm hosting a parade when hardship comes my way. But I don't have to tackle these difficulties alone either. I can share my concerns with God. He's always willing to help lighten my load. I can let Him make these unlikely gifts part of His plan for me.

I pull God into every situation. "Get up a minute, will you?"

I snap His beach chair shut and drag it a little closer to the action. "Here is better," I say.

I go back to the field and take my position in the game. I like to glance over and see His face. It's not enough to just assume He's somewhere in the crowd.

I give Him a wave. I can actually see Him mouthing the words, "Pay attention."

God is my biggest fan.

Sometimes, I'm in a hurry. Every day, there's so much to get done. I find myself pushing God to the bottom of the list. And then, I feel guilty. I add this feeling to the pile of chores that need my attention.

Quick prayers count:

> I love you, Lord.
>
> I feel your presence.
>
> Help me, Jesus.
>
> Thank you.

God has tons of things to do. But no matter what, He always makes time for me. I have no idea how He does it. I guess it's not necessary that I solve this mystery. All I know is that I'm grateful.

When I keep my dreams small and manageable, I can actually see them in my mind. I collect these thoughts and place them in God's lap.

With His blessings, they become goals.

Everybody has something to say. Comments fly around in the air like frantic birds. Life gets so noisy, and I'm easily influenced by all these points of view.

When I feel overwrought, I'm glad that I know how to comfort myself without escaping from my thoughts. I reach for that blanket of calm and listen for God's voice amidst the chatter. Sometimes, He sounds like Morgan Freeman. Other times, Mr. Carson from Downton Abbey.

Either way—in the soothing quiet, I can readjust my thinking. I don't have to get caught up in the world's opinions.

God has a plan for my life.

But I have all these ambitions. Some of them are big and good. Others are absurd.

When I'm determined to get my way, I leave God out. I don't mean to. Well, maybe I do. I want what I want, after all.

Help me, Lord, to come to you first with my ideas. So we can look at them together and make smart choices. So you can guide my energy and help me curb my appetite for excess.

My friends, my husband and children surround me with decency. They reflect myself back to me in virtuous ways. This is no accident. Good people come my way for important reasons.

For a long time, I chose my companions and boyfriends indiscriminately. I was lonely and desperate. One man in particular liked to smoke PCP and tear the place to pieces. He beat my ass, and I let him. Because he was so fucked up, I felt better about the things I did. I wasn't as bad off as him.

That kind of thinking isn't right. Or fair. I wasn't a victim. I knew he was troubled when I invited him into my life.

I was moved when I found out he hung himself. I read about it in the news. I have a feeling he never got clean. I pray for him sometimes. I like to think he is in Heaven. It doesn't serve me well to resent his memory.

I'm just grateful I got out. God is very good to me. I want to be good too.

I felt like I could never go to another party again. Or get dressed up. Or listen to the radio. I decided these things were over for me, and I was sad.

Realistically, it had been so long since I'd gone out socially where I wasn't preoccupied with how much liquor there was. And if they'd run out. Sneaking around to get wired so no one would know. I couldn't concentrate on a song to save my life. Or conversation.

When I first got sober, I didn't know how to do anything— not fucked up.

God helps out with all these difficulties. I didn't have to confront any of it on my own. Or right away. Or ever. I had nothing to prove except that I wanted to live. And even with that, there was no pressure. Nobody could make me stop getting high. It was my choice.

Today, I'm healthy, safe and free. I clean up real nice. Parties are so much fun. And music is awesome. I still like to play it loud.

If I had to wait and use just the right words in order to speak with God, He'd probably never hear from me.

At any given moment, there's such a vast assortment of thoughts and feelings swirling around on the inside. I hardly ever know exactly what it is I want to say before I say it. Do you?

I just usually start talking. About whatever. I get to the point sooner or later. And if I don't, it still feels right.

I love when God and I are together.

I used to hide when the telephone rang. The unscheduled interruptions always threw me for a loop.

"What the hell does he want?" I asked myself. "Can't she just leave me alone?"

I listened to the concerned voices on the answering machine. I tried to figure out if folks were worried or angry. But I wouldn't return any calls.

Unless, of course, I was loaded. Then, I could bend your ear for hours. I might even dial you up late at night and want to bullshit forever. I saw nothing inappropriate with midnight conversations. I was ready to chat, and you needed to make yourself available.

The next morning, I might only remember bits and pieces of what we discussed. Embarrassed, I'd avoid you for months.

Once I got sober, I had to learn how to communicate on the phone like a reasonable person. Leave messages that made sense. Request information and wait patiently for responses.

Today when a friend checks in and I miss the call, I ring her back promptly. I realize life is busy and there's never enough time to catch up the way I'd like. But communication is what keeps relationships healthy and relevant.

Whenever I decide that my happiness hinges on getting stuff in order to feel good, my serenity is at risk. Waiting on what I want so I can enjoy certain emotions is unnatural. Plus, I become a miserable bitch in the meanwhile, and no one is safe.

I hate putting my desires on hold. I get anxious, and I can't concentrate. The only thing I seem capable of is worry—another useless attempt at manipulating the outcome.

What if my plans don't work out? Then, not only am I disappointed, but I will have wasted all that time wishing for something that wasn't meant for me to begin with.

Forget being happy. I'll just feel foolish and resentful. God help anybody who just happens to be passing by. They won't even know what hit them.

Happiness can be such a beautiful experience, if allowed to develop on its own. I really shouldn't try and mess with it.

I got invited to do stuff, and I truly wanted to go places with friends. I quickly said, "Yes, yes, yes!" But as social engagements came closer to actually happening, I almost always flaked. This was me:

"That baby shower is just too far to get to."

"I don't have money to buy a gift."

"I've got nothing nice to wear."

None of these mitigating circumstances were particularly valid. It's just that real pleasure threatened my drinking and drug use.

I watched the clock tick past the start time for each occasion. I hated myself for not being able to do anything but get drunk and snort away my evenings. I obsessed about the life I wasn't living.

In my mind, I began creating excuses for why I couldn't make it. Elaborate stories that justified my absence. Someone was sick and needed my help. Perhaps a robbery or a fire at the pet shop.

I wanted folks to know that I really would have been there... Had it not been for that terrible accident where I had to save all those imaginary people and their animals from danger. And subsequently miss the party. Sorry.

I leaned on my dramatic pretend world as if it were real. I wondered if anyone actually believed me. I made sure to mention my heroic deeds and misadventures again and again.

Even when every word that left my mouth was a lie, I wanted the world to know I was important and necessary. Even though I didn't feel like either of those things. I didn't have very much purpose. Except for going home, cracking open that giant bottle of wine and getting with my dope.

I never, ever bragged about that.

Today, I'm glad that I can admit these faults without shame. In my sober life, I get to do so many meaningful things. My mind is clear to simply concentrate on all the joy. Commitment has become reflexive, and so has the follow-through.

I have a habit of gauging my own self-image by the successes and failures of my contemporaries. I look at what somebody else is doing, how he and she carry themselves and I wish it were me. I make comparisons to what other people have.

Heaven help you ladies if you own a cute little handbag that turns my head. Or a shiny piece of jewelry I'd love to see on my wrist or finger. Envy can get my mind in a real twist.

But wait, there's more. I also judge folks whose behavior is less than ideal.

Shame on them, I think to myself.

Shit, I may even say it out loud. I might mention it to my husband or a girlfriend if what's been done really rubs me the wrong way. As if every move I make is perfect and exemplary. As if God went on vacation and left me in charge.

Of course, this isn't right. I know it's none of my business what other folks do, but that doesn't stop me from acting this way. Superficial details are notorious for influencing my decisions and opinions of myself and others.

Lord, I need a hand with this kind of imprudence. I realize you're always trying to help me appreciate that I am me, and they are them. And that my authentic happiness comes from what already exists in my life.

I guess what I'm trying to say is this… Thank you. I know you're doing the very best you can with what you've got to work with. Me.

I woke up this morning with lots to do. Another hectic schedule filled with goals and commitments. Everybody needs something, and I've got to make it happen.

Before I put my feet on the floor, I turn my thoughts to my Higher Power. I envision Him sitting on the chair next to my bed.

"How did you sleep?" God asks.

"Lord, I slept very well. I'm ready to start my day."

"I'm so glad," He replies. "I love to just watch over you while you rest. It's a very peaceful time, when you are dreaming and perfectly still."

I like remembering that God is always with me. Especially before I fling the blankets aside and spring into action.

God is always holding my hand, even when it gets sweaty.

If ever I complain, He just switches sides. But He never lets go.

I love being able to concentrate on stuff. I couldn't focus on anything worth a damn when I was using. I wanted to, but it's like my brain wouldn't let me. It just ran around, chasing shiny objects all over the place, like a frantic cat.

A speedy mind may feel like energy, but it's not. I never got one legitimate thing accomplished that's worth talking about. And if I did manage to get close to finishing something I started, I was moving way too fast to appreciate the importance of what was going on. I sure as hell don't remember the details.

Drugs aren't real. They're just a trick. From the very first time I started taking them, they faked me out. It doesn't make me love them any less. But man, what a rip off.

You wouldn't have been able to explain any of this stuff to me when I was getting high. I was quicker and smarter than everyone.

Good Lord, I am so happy to be free.

I thought the speed would help curb my appetite. I seldom felt hungry. And if I drank my dinner away, all the better! I didn't need food. I made up my own rules.

I wanted to join a gym, but I never had enough money. Besides, my evenings were devoted exclusively to getting trashed. There was no time for fitness. I found myself on an exercise bike in my sister's basement—with a wine glass in my hand and a tissue full of pills tucked inside my bra. I was working out!

My heart tightens just a little bit whenever I reflect on memories like this one. My behavior made absolutely no sense. But it did when I was using, and it would if I picked up again. I'd be running for office in Crazy Town before I drained that first bottle. I know this to be true.

The image of me pedaling that stationary bicycle right off a cliff helps me remember how close I came to truly losing my mind.

It took a lot of energy and creative focus to get high every day. To drink every night. To scrape myself off the floor in the morning and do it all over again. That's some powerful determination right there.

Obsessions can be transformed through recovery. My uncontrollable urges have become a new enthusiasm for life. An opportunity for growth. A saving grace.

I believe in my sobriety. And God. And myself.
When I think of all these neat things, I can't help but say "Yippee!"

What an important morning!

I've prepared my two children for their sleepaway adventure. They have everything they need. Clothing, bug spray, flashlights and comic books. Together, we will drive two hours into the mountains of North Carolina—to the camp location. They are beyond excited, and I am thrilled for them.

My boys do not worry about me when they are away. It never even enters their minds. They do bring envelopes and stamps, however. I may get a letter that arrives a week or two after their return. That always makes me smile.

They focus exclusively on their carefree summer, as they should. It is a glorious time to observe their lives as they develop into fine young men and create memories that will last forever.

Tonight, Dave and I will watch our TV shows without interruption. I may even eat potato chips in my bed. It will be outstanding.

I am thinking clearly, and I am grateful. This moment exists as a shining example of the miracle of recovery.

As I go through my daily list of Things to Do, I try to tackle the most significant items first. I know exactly what they are because they press the heaviest against the walls of my mind. I shouldn't put these things off.

Why carry all that extra weight around if I don't have to? I just need to direct my attention to the important jobs that need to get done—before I start resenting them unnecessarily.

When someone makes a suggestion on my behalf, I try to catch myself before I reply, "I know, but…"

All that ever really means is "I'm not ready to change."

I have dreams now. And although not crystal clear by definition, they are real.

These images are not the same as the vague, misguided notions that once skittered across the surface of my drunken thoughts, provoking me to tears and angry outbursts, forgotten in the morning.

My dreams are located safely in my heart. I refer to them all the time. They have substance and add value to my life. They direct me toward my goals. I feel smart knowing I've chosen these ambitions for myself.

I am no longer afraid of or intimidated by my great ideas.

Sometimes when I'm doing my chores, my mind drifts to thoughts of trying to trick someone else into doing my chores.

But I know they wouldn't be done right. And then, I'd be crabbier than ever.

So instead, I just concentrate on getting them over with. And then, I can return to feeling good. Knowing that I won't have to address these chores again until tomorrow.

They always had enough volunteers to clean up at the end of the meetings. If I was going to offer my help, I'd wait for no hands to be raised. So I could jump in and show them how great I was. I wanted to do all the jobs by myself, ensuring maximum glory. Stacking chairs and throwing away trash like nobody's business.

But by then, everyone would have said goodbye and left. Driving off to resume their sober lives. Leaving me behind with piles of work—like usual. That's how I operated in my head, alone in a bubble of martyrdom and resentment.

One of the most valuable lessons I've learned in recovery is the beauty and strength of a group effort. I can fold up my own chair and a few others when the meeting is over. Quietly gather spent coffee cups.

I do my part. Other folks are doing the same thing.

I smile at friendly faces in the doorway. And then, off I go. I want to belong to something bigger than myself. It helps me retain my right size.

Deep in the throes of my drinking and drug use, I watched the world from a remote location. Like a lonely spectator. Despite the fact that I left folks hanging and caused considerable damage, I was disconnected from the action. I slipped away from any involvement and disappeared inside my own mind.

I was paranoid and defensive. I didn't know how to make decisions. Instead, I reacted to the decisions being made all around me. I never dreamed I'd regain my footing. I couldn't imagine what that might look like.

Every day I'm sober is a gift, a step in the right direction. I have opportunities to participate in my life and contribute to what's happening. Even when things are stressful, I can feel my feelings and not freak out. I appreciate being present and accountable.

God stood at my door and knocked. "Mary, why don't you let me in?"

"I can't, Lord. I've done all these fucked up things."

"I know," He replied. "That's why I'm here."

I tried to get everyone to love me. I became whatever person I thought friends wanted to hang out with. I had so many different identities, I completely lost sight of who I was and what I liked to do.

I thought the whole world was watching me, and it was my job to provide the entertainment. When people were partying, I was thrilled. I liked getting wasted, and I was very good at it. Drinking and doping around were easy ways for me to fit in.

Until I began suspecting I was trapped and couldn't get out. I watched folks move on and pursue things they enjoyed. Being loaded was my only interest. And it had become a mandatory prerequisite.

In recovery, I am much more at ease with my identity. I'm learning how to explore what it means to be me. I celebrate my unique qualities and talents. I can share them with confidence, when I feel it's appropriate.

I still get nervous in some social situations. And I won't lie, I really dig when people like me. But I don't feel the need to bend over backwards the way I used to. I can also guarantee I'm much better company without a drink in my hand.

I practice happy thinking every day.

That doesn't mean I flop about, behaving like a lunatic. But I do make the effort to contribute positive thoughts.

Not everybody digs this scene. But generally, the feedback is quite favorable.

My emotions were a mess, and they drove me in all directions—demanding more pleasure and satisfaction than I deserved. I was so heavily focused on how people mistreated and neglected me. I was never wrong.

When it came time to examine my character defects, I didn't know what to expect. Taking on this huge gray area of behavioral turmoil and assigning explanations for every natural desire that had become warped and unreasonable. I couldn't do this exercise on my own.

Remarkably, it felt good to finally admit that I'd been irresponsible and dishonest. Yes, I was unfaithful and manipulative in my relationships. I was a devious busybody and a coward. I'd denied all these negative qualities.

I researched character flaws—and there they were, officially in print. I went through the huge list, checking off every fault that pertained to me. How liberating. And what a relief that I didn't have all of them. Just a handful, really.

I discussed these unbecoming features with my sponsor. She told me what some of hers were. Interestingly enough, I wouldn't trade mine for anyone else's.

As soon as I allowed this information as truth, I felt better. That blanket of shame was lifted, and I started looking at these shortcomings in a pragmatic way.

Instead of feeling like I couldn't do anything about them except lie and pretend they weren't there.

Many of my defects have lessened as my mental and spiritual health continues to improve. I will always have weaknesses that make me feel vulnerable. But at least now, I can identify what they are. And work toward responding with positivity.

I cannot say 'yes' to every situation, however flattering.

Come on over. Let's meet. Would love for you to be there.

Casual invites that sound like lots of fun. And they are. I'm thrilled when folks request my company.

But so many becomes too many in a minute. I lose my balance and begin to feel resentful. I can't think straight with all the social commitments I've agreed to.

I always pray that God helps me with this. He knows I struggle saying 'no.' I'd like to do all these fabulous things, and I don't want to hurt anybody's feelings.

But it's important that I keep it simple. Life remains harmonious. And I can be a much better friend this way.

Days are supposed to begin and end—with action occurring in the middle and rest in between for energy. These lines became incomprehensibly blurred because I wanted and needed to get high. Addiction made it impossible to acknowledge, let alone respect, most boundaries.

I pushed my brain and body beyond its natural limits. It seemed like I was always awake, but not really there. My exhaustion became something so terrifying, I was scared to close my eyes. It was like I'd forgotten how, and I didn't deserve sleep because of what I was doing.

I dreaded the night and everything it represented for me. Huge plastic cups of cheap box wine, cocaine, pills and vague, self-prescribed heartache.

I really don't miss staying up all hours, agonizing over situations I couldn't change. Manipulating people in my mind. Among other things, the loneliness was fucking killing me.

I want to do something useful with these memories. Because I can't forget any of this stuff and pretend like it didn't happen.

That's not how staying sober works for me. I need to talk to other people about the changes in my life. Tell my stories and hear theirs. Share this powerful message—that a way out is within reach.

Today, I live all the joy and creativity that eluded me for years. I am productive and energetic. My heart feels safe, and at bedtime, I sleep like a baby.

I've made the decision it's not just okay that folks know I'm an addict and alcoholic in recovery. It's really important. I am what 'being restored to sanity' looks like. This is how the good news spreads.

When I focus on something, I'm leading my mind in a specific direction, where life will be impacted by the decisions I make. Wow. What a trip!

But sometimes, I don't realize I'm going the wrong way. And even if I do, my pride prevents me from stopping the vehicle. People, trees and buildings keep whizzing past, and I just continue on. I can get hopelessly lost before I know it.

Having God along for the ride is smart planning. Because even though I'm responsible for my future, not everything proceeds as outlined on the map. There will still be disappointments and bumps in the road. Weather conditions and potential car trouble.

God is the ideal companion. He is level-headed and knows exactly where I'm going. He takes up virtually no space. When I include Him in my thoughts and actions, the smallest things become more meaningful.

"Take a look at that sky," He might suggest. "Isn't it something?"

"Did you notice how pleasant that clerk in the gas station was?"

"Why don't you let those kids cross the street first? We're not in that big a hurry."

My journey is a sublime experience. And there's never a reason for me to travel alone.

I try to be specific when I talk to God. So He knows exactly what I need.

"Lord, please let there be one banana left in the kitchen this morning. If not, I will gladly eat something else. But a banana for my cereal sure would be nice."

It doesn't make sense to hide the truth from myself. I'll have to deal with reality sooner or later anyway. So why waste time?

I ask God for the courage to help me face facts. To respond honestly. To try and be kind. My behavior could be the catalyst for someone else's truth.

I am a wolf, and I will always be a wolf.

But today, I am determined to not eat any sheep.

Yesterday is done. Its power is gone. Yet it still serves a unique purpose.

Yesterday shines a gentle, generous light on all of my failures. Sure, they happened. There's no denying it. But I can turn to them as lessons. They are solid examples of all the things I never have to do again, as long as I don't pick up.

Today is here. Shiny, new choices are mine.

When I was done running around, both physically and mentally finished with my own personal war, I couldn't stand myself anymore. I felt inhumanly fearful and completely out-of-control. I kept peering over my shoulder at all the damage I'd done.

I stared into the smoldering ash of a life incinerated by drugs and alcohol. I sifted through the rubble for scraps of something worth saving. I was ashamed and disgusted every waking moment. And all I wanted to do was get high.

As time went on and I put a few days together, I started to feel a little better. I'd gotten some rest. My head no longer throbbed, and I was well-fed. My husband hadn't left me. I personally thought I would sleep and eat myself to death. Such was the extent of my paranoia.

And still, I wanted to get high. Because it's all I knew. My body demonstrated that it could heal itself, but my mind begged for relief from the stress of exposure to a world where I had no tools for survival. I was the most scared I've ever been.

Today, things are different. I am clean and sober. I have God in my life, the love of a good man and a strong program of recovery that I take very seriously. I have people who care about my well-being, my feelings and goals for the future. I depend on a vibrant community of friends who understand my situation and support me in my progress.

And they, in turn, depend on me. I love that.

I am grateful and eager to share what I know. I celebrate the on-going message of hope.

I didn't realize these were the things I would want. But they certainly are everything I need.

When my supply ran low, the whole world became a heavy presence. People kept moving and talking, but I didn't care about what. It was almost as if the sound was completely turned off. The only thing that mattered was getting more. I needed back on that ride.

And once I scored, I could breathe again. Catch up to the others or tune them out—whichever direction I wanted to travel with my high. I decided which way to go. I was in charge. Ha!

How could I have thought such a thing? All that preparation took time and energy. First, I needed to pull myself away from what was left. Make phone calls and borrow money. Meet up to buy dope and get my drink. Come back and return to the business of quiet self-destruction.

I thought about these memories earlier while I chauffeured my young sons to the comic book store. I listened to their innocent conversation as they sat in the backseats of my car, trusting my every move. Neither boy has ever seen me loaded. I am humbled by this phenomenon.

"How about you?" one of them inquired as I drove.

"How about me, what?"

"C'mon, Mom. Weren't you paying attention?"

"I guess not."

"What were you thinking about?"

"Something important," I said.

"Tell us."

"Nah. Why don't you just tell me what I missed?"

God has big dreams for me.

I really need to clear out some of the crap in my mind so He has somewhere to put them.

Oh, man. I am flawed.

I make mistakes. I get frustrated and lose my temper. I have resentments.

And still, God loves me.

There are lots of things I can't explain. No one says I have to. It's just not necessary.

I don't always know the right thing to do.

But I'm getting a whole lot better at recognizing what the wrong thing looks like.

Yesterday can be rough. It's always gonna be there.

But it's not today anymore, and that has to count for something.

My disease is such a piece of work.

"Don't feel bad about picking up," it likes to whisper as I'm sitting in meetings, waiting for my turn to share. "It's not that big a deal. Besides, the people in this group are so nice, and everybody loves you. They've all been there. You know they'll forgive you. This is a safe place."

My addiction misses me so much.

Here's another angle it likes to work...

"Listen, Mary. If you get high, what a total shock it will be for these folks. You know, somebody like you—with so many years clean. You could show them just how easy it is to slip. You'd be setting a solid example of what not to do."

"And then, you can come back, all sorry and shit. Start again, and get stronger than ever. Relapses really strengthen an addict's resolve."

What a manipulative bitch my disease is. I never want us to get back together.

Situations may occur only once, but I tend to replay them over and over in my mind until they feel humongous.

God knows I do this. He helps me sort out all the extra echoes and shadows, so I can deal with things in their actual size. Effectively. And get back to being peaceful and productive.

When I was drinking and carrying on, my life was filled with fights and fallouts. I was in perpetual battle mode. I took on boyfriends, neighbors, bosses, strangers. Every single person on earth was out to get me, and I had to be ready.

It's not like I understood how to communicate my thoughts or exercise any self-control. I didn't know what it meant to mind my own business. I just jumped into the ring as soon as I heard the bell.

I don't remember ever winning one argument. That's because I was always drunk, my opinions never made any sense, and I flat out sucked at fighting. I got my clock cleaned on a regular basis. I could never figure out where I went wrong.

Today, I let go of my need to be involved in altercations. If someone wants to get into it with me, the smartest move I can make is to simply walk away. I'm grateful my legs aren't broken. I like to keep them that way.

Quieting my mind is like getting all the tigers at the circus to stand on their hind legs at the same time.

It takes a few tries. But when it finally happens, what a thrill!

There are some nights when I'm sleeping, I dream about it. And in these dreams, I am back to the business of destroying my life.

I feel devious and paranoid. I'm doing things I know I shouldn't. I lie to cover it all up—because I'm so smart. I can probably fix this quick, before anybody finds out.

But my mind is floating in slumber, and I have no control. I tell myself that I'm drunk and high, and everything is perfect. I recall that perfect feeling. And maybe for a second, it is exactly as I remember.

The rest of the time is dreadful. I am back to running and hiding, stealing people's shit and leaving folks in the lurch. My disappointment is catastrophic, and the shame is very real. Every move I make turns these ethereal thoughts into all-out nightmares.

What a relief it is to wake up, to realize it was just a dream. And everything is still okay. Thank God, everything is okay.

When life presents challenges that are too big for me to handle on my own, I turn toward the house and call God's name.

"Hey, my ball's in the street!" I yell up at the window. "You said I should come get you when that happens."

The Lord opens the screen and leans His elbows on the ledge. "Only if you feel you're not ready to do things by yourself," He reminds me.

"Oh, I forgot."

"Well, are you ready?"

I pause to consider this question. I look into God's knowing face and feel the warmth of His love, His patience.

"It's already in my hand, isn't it?" I ask.

He waves and goes back inside. I return to bouncing my ball against the stoop.

God not only has the answer. He *is* the answer.

I am conscious of the way I speak to myself, especially when I encounter a difficult situation or I'm learning something new.

The private conversations that occur inside my head can help clarify my thoughts. "I know exactly what's going on here." They can also motivate me when I lack confidence. "I can do this!"

I try to keep my comments positive, as I would with a friend. I treat myself with kindness and respect because that's what I deserve.

As I continue to stay sober, I look forward to making all kinds of progress.

In my relationships and personal goals, my spiritual life, I feel strong and capable. My dreams are big and colorful! But I have no idea how and when these changes will occur. I can't turn my expectations into demands. Oh, how I want to.

All I can do is trust in God. Address my side of the street. Have faith that everything is exactly as it should be. Right at this moment.

I am determined to get and stay acquainted with the Real Me.

I don't try to control behavior that isn't mine.

Two arms, two legs, one head and a heart. These are my basic parts. The equipment I use to make good things happen.

I breathe, think and move through my day and the world.

I am a simple creature. I am responsible for me.

The truth is never bad, no matter what it is. The truth is just there, as an occurrence. It's all the negativity that latches onto that truth. That's what makes everything crazy and turns situations into drama.

When I let go of all the opinions, good and bad, the truth just stands there—cool as a cucumber. Smoking a cigarette and quietly flicking the butt into the street. It really doesn't want any trouble.

God either is or He isn't, and I get to choose. It's a very simple concept, but the details feel enormous.

When I try to think things through, I find myself saying, "Whoa," out loud. But in a calm and qualified voice. "Whoa."

I just love thoughts like these.

Every evening, I couldn't wait for the world to just leave me alone. So I could start the pour and fill myself with wine, tumbler after tumbler.

Dope to perk up, and pills to come down. Lost in the sauce. This is how I peeled away the day.

And every morning, I clung to the night before. Heartbroken that it was over. Grief-stricken even. My crumpled body, crawling back into motion with flat soda and more pills. Drugs as soon as I could get them. And then, my beloved drink.

I don't want to live that way anymore. Or ever again.

I love my cautious freedom. I am so thankful that I no longer depend on the old patterns of behavior to govern my decisions. I wake up ready to apply my mind and body productively.

I like to pause before I get going, just to recognize all that I have.

My whole life, I have been driven by extremes. But I've come to appreciate that moderation is key to a peaceful Mary. Simple gestures have such tremendous impact on the quality of my life.

A balanced diet, so I don't feel sluggish from eating crap all day. Enough sleep that I can embrace my chores and responsibilities without feeling sorry for myself. Or behaving like a bitch and ripping people's heads off. Exercise for stamina to keep up with my children and not look so scary at the pool. My thighs, yuck.

I also make sure my body is clean. It's a great way to perk up as well as relax. I'm in the shower at least twice a day because I don't get high anymore. I do what works. Besides, the world deserves good smells.

And I pray. I know God loves hearing from me. I always feel better when I check in.

I rather enjoy this new awareness. I have moments where I truly feel like I understand what's going on in my mind. And everything is okay. The confusion lifts naturally. I'm at ease with my emotions. It's almost as if I'm discovering a brand new person. Only familiar. Hey, I'll take it.

This serenity does pass, though. I'm thrown off dozens of times during the course of the day. But I can get it back again. I have tools and techniques that I use, friends I turn to for help.

I used to think by getting wasted, I was enhancing my perception of the world. Providing myself with a unique interpretation of life's rich pageant. Deluxe accommodations. What bullshit. All I did was get plastered. It's not a special skill.

The only way to be clear about things is to be clear. Stay brave and sober. Live life. I'm going with that.

I can talk pretty tough. But I'm not tough.

Deep down, I'm a yellow chicken. Conflict scares me. Change is terrifying. I'm afraid of failure and the possibility of looking stupid. Then, there's loneliness and rejection.

Fear was always the engine that drove my addictions. Drinking and snorting dope made it easy to escape from awkward feelings and situations. But I never really managed my fear. It was still there when I sobered up. Only bigger and more insistent.

In recovery, I am learning new ways to handle being afraid. I don't want to just avoid the things that frighten me. Now, I push through the discomfort and actually deal with shit. I dispatch threats tactfully. I don't get mixed up in drama that's not mine. Interestingly enough, I don't generate a whole lot of drama anymore. My life is rather tranquil. Imagine.

Still, I like that I'm free to take risks if I choose to. I can challenge myself. I have lots of cool dreams. And the clarity to dream them.

God is my best friend. It's pretty intense.

Sure, I have other friends, and we are close. But this thing I have with God isn't like other relationships.

I can tell God everything without having to explain my feelings. All I have to do is think about Him. This is helpful because sometimes, I'm not even sure what's going on. Perhaps my mind is confused, and my heart is a bit distraught. But when I keep Him close and include Him in the details, I feel better.

God is always thrilled to hear from me. I can share my whole day with Him. The big news that fills me with joy. The boring minutiae that clutters my head and sours my mood. He doesn't expect a parade. Nor should I.

Life doesn't have to be perfect for it to be beautiful.

Sometimes, my memories make me sad. I have told the most preposterous lies. I robbed folks and left them wondering where their shit went. I helped them look for it. I let innocent people take the blame. I brought violent storms of worry into otherwise peaceful lives. I've done a lot of things I wish I hadn't.

But I cannot live in my regret. I know I'm not perfect. I just need to keep moving forward. And be the person I want to become. There is hope and room in the world for me. I feel it.

I have to begin somewhere, so I choose right here and now. Every new day brings a fresh start and opportunities to recreate myself.

I'm so grateful my mother taught me how to pray. How to turn to God when things get rough. And thank Him for the gifts He's given me.

She may not have mastered all the instructions, but neither have I.

I think Mom did a great job. I totally get the message. Granted, our relationship wasn't perfect. Still, I know she'd be so pleased with the woman I've become.

I have always been willful. Even when this energy blasted my potential to pieces, tore my relationships apart and nearly killed me—I wanted my way.

Now that I'm sober, I am learning how to convert this willfulness into persistence. How to harness my strengths and move toward my objectives.

Persistent preparation keeps the drama to a minimum. Persistent efforts become good reflexes. Persistent prayer brings me closer to God and helps me realize that all things are possible in faith.

I am in charge of the world I create for myself. I find that I am making sound decisions that serve me well. But I don't always know the right way to behave. I pop off sometimes. I am human.

Before I respond to any situation that may bring difficulty or conflict into my life, I try to think things through and consider my options. I mean really envision a fair and practical approach. I talk to folks who offer good insight and have my best interests at heart. I spend time with God so He can influence my thoughts and actions.

I remind myself that everything will be okay, and this is a very nice world I live in. Then I proceed with a clear conscience and the knowledge that I've made smart choices before, and I can do it again.

I move toward that reasonable outcome and hope for the best.

Because God loves me, He gives me all these spectacular blessings. A great life, sturdy relationships, healthy children, a promising future.

Other perks, too. Adorable shoes on sale, interesting conversations with friends, TV shows I think are clever. Whenever my hair comes out just right.

I can easily get worked up by all these bells and whistles. I start coming to God with my list of demands.

"I'm gonna need friendly people everywhere I go, Lord. No traffic ever. Compliments and lots of them. Plus, half-n-half for the coffee. If we've got no cream, I might just tear this place to ribbons."

Prayer brings me back to what really matters: My relationship with God. When I stay close to Him, I feel safe and centered and focused. Praying helps me shake off all the distractions, so I can tune in to what's important.

Keeping things simple.

It's not my favorite thing to do, but I can be humble.

And I have an open mind.

These are the helpful tools I use to get close and stay close to God. He is restoring my sanity. It happens in little bits and big chunks.

I can't decide these measures. That's His job.

"I am good enough… Just the way I am."

I say these words aloud, and they sound even more ridiculous.

"I am good enough… Just the way I am."

I search for "self-worth" in the dictionary. Just to be sure I know exactly what it is that I'm looking for. Self-worth is the sense of my own value as a person. That sounds magnificent. So, yes. I would like that very much. More, please.

"I am good enough… Just the way I am."

Little by little, I can learn how to trust my own truth.

I dare myself to be still. To flip the big switch that shuts everything down. All the machines, the whirring sounds and flashing lights that make my brain and body go. And go. And go. And go.

I have things to do and places to get to. I am busy and important. I'll never finish on time, and I can't stop right now.

Sure, I can. Just for a second. Stop. Just to say "Hey" and "Thanks." Maybe more, once I settle. And realize that the world isn't gonna end if I take a deep breath and listen for God's voice.

In the quiet of a prayerful moment, everything can change. And anything can happen.

That's where it happens for me.

Hanging out with God is like having a job at the record store.

Sure, there are challenges and responsibility, with lots of work to be done. But for the most part, it's the ideal environment.

Plus, I get to wear whatever I want. And choose the music.

I need to do things on my own.

Which means I can't blame anyone else for my mistakes.
They're all mine.

And that's okay. I'm learning about things. I'm making
decisions. I'm growing in ways I could never imagine.

I allow thoughts to take up space in my mind. They hang out on the stoop, right beyond my brain.

Some of them are friendly and get along with everything else that's going on up there. They stick around for a little while, and then move on. They mean well and have smart purpose.

Other thoughts are punks and pains in the ass. They linger at the bottom of the steps, with nowhere to go. They eat Doritos and drink blue soda. They leave their garbage everywhere. They dip in and out of my conscience, and I feel uneasy. They pretend they don't see me when I try to get past.

"Can you move?" I ask nicely.

"Make me."

It is a challenge, but I can do it. Even though I'm afraid to confront these unpleasant situations, I'm responsible for what goes on in my head. I own the building. I get to choose what kind of thoughts spend time on my property.

This is how I stay centered and balanced throughout the day. I use my broom to keep my side of the street clean.

When I let go of negativity, my whole body relaxes and I am calm.

It's an amazing feeling, but it does not come naturally.

I have to practice releasing my reflex for tension and disappointment.

I can only address one specific idea at a time.

I'm pretty sure that's how most brains work. Mine takes care of each individual request, dispatches commands and moves on to the next. Other notions wait in the queue until it is their turn. Or they push ahead like assholes.

When I was trying to get clean very early on, like in the first few days, my cravings came up hard and rough to the front of the line. Every second, every space was filled with the pressure of these manic thoughts.

It went on this way for what felt like forever. All the shoving and grabbing for attention. Making trouble for other parts of my body so I would let them through.

I remember concentrating on my brain like it was a piece of machinery. I imagined a big dude standing in this narrow doorway, holding a wand like at the airport. Just trying to do his job.

In my mind, I emptied all my thoughts into a bucket and placed them on a conveyer belt so they could get scanned. It may sound silly, but this image helped me slow my reactions down. Until I had thirty minutes, half a day, 24 hours. And then, a week under my belt.

I wonder sometimes if God wishes I could be quieter.
Listen better and not run my mouth so much.

But He's just too nice to say anything.

Those first few gulps of coffee are just extraordinary. I send them into my body to perform a specific task. Wake everything up!

Some mornings, I hold the cup to my face and rest its warm surface against my lips and cheek.

I close my eyes and think about all the friends I have everywhere. I love when folks want to be my friend. It appeals to the part of me that will forever be twelve.

I envision us enjoying our coffee together.

I acknowledge and accept the person I have been. Yes, I did some things. I was there. That was me.

I take a nice deep breath. I say my prayers and move forward.

As I continue to build a new life in recovery, I focus on the windows. Not the walls.

My hangovers compelled me to gobble aspirin and Tylenol as if it were powder-coated candy that tasted like shit.

Then, I'd throw everything up and have to start all over again.

I can't recall the last headache I had that required pills to make it go away.

Remembering this is helpful.

Continue to open my heart, Lord. Help me to love the way you do.

It would suck to miss out on something amazing because I'm afraid. Or unsure of exactly what it is that I have to offer. How will I ever know unless I try?

Guide my efforts and energy toward folks who need me, just as I need them. I may not always recognize what these opportunities look like.

Let's help each other however we can.

Let's travel together. It'll be fun.

Let's share the news about a better way to live.

Yes, we should remember where we've been. Still, let's celebrate where we're going.

Let's see how many of us we can fit inside my uncle's station wagon. We'll probably have to make a few trips, but so what?

Everything is possible with a clear head, a willing heart and our favorite songs on the radio.

I have something to give, and so do you.

When we tell our stories and share what we're learning, we touch one another in valuable ways. There are messages in every experience—the best and the worst. Everything becomes more meaningful when we connect.

Thank you for making a difference. For being such a thoughtful presence in my life. In those moments that become my day.

I am grateful we are friends.

How is it possible that I can be the same person as when I was using? When everything in my life has changed, and nothing appears as it once was?

How is it possible that I like what I see when I look in the mirror? And that the memories that once contributed to my self-destruction now illuminate my path as I move forward?

I have a feeling faith pulls these questions together. Faith gives me just enough peace, so I don't really need the answers spelled out for me. I can just take a few deep breaths and appreciate my progress.

Still, I keep praying and thinking and hoping and sharing. I can totally do that. I stay committed to my recovery because it's the most precious thing in the world to me.